HBJ SOCIAL STUDIES

FAMILIES

LANDMARK EDITION

Stephanie Abraham Hirsh, Ph.D.
GENERAL EDITOR

Phillip Bacon, Ph.D.
SENIOR EDITORIAL ADVISER

HBJ HARCOURT BRACE JOVANOVICH, PUBLISHERS
Orlando   San Diego   Chicago   Dallas

GENERAL EDITOR

Dr. Stephanie Abraham Hirsh is Director of Program and Staff Development for the Richardson Independent School District in Richardson, Texas. Dr. Hirsh has a B.S. degree from the University of Texas at Austin, an M.Ed. from North Texas State University, and a Ph.D. in Curriculum and Instruction from North Texas State University. In addition to her work within the school district, Dr. Hirsh has served as a consultant for social studies and staff development, has taught university courses, and has published numerous articles in several educational journals. Dr. Hirsh is a past president of the Texas Council for the Social Studies. She serves currently on the Executive Board of the Social Studies Supervisors Association and numerous committees for the National Council for the Social Studies.

SENIOR EDITORIAL ADVISER

Dr. Phillip Bacon is a professor Emeritus of Geography and Anthropology at the University of Houston. Dr. Bacon has also served on the faculties of Columbia University and the University of Washington. Formerly Dean of the Graduate School of Peabody College for Teachers at Vanderbilt University, Dr. Bacon began his career in education as a teacher of elementary and secondary social studies. He is the author or editor of more than 36 books, including the *Life Pictorial Atlas of the World*. For 18 years, Dr. Bacon served as a member of the Editorial Advisory Board of *World Book Encyclopedia*.

Among his numerous honors and awards, Dr. Bacon holds the distinguished titles of Fellow of the Explorers Club and Fellow of the Royal Geographic Society of Great Britain. He is a three-time recipient of the Teaching Excellence Award at the University of Houston. His biography appears in *Who's Who in America* and *American Men and Women in Science*.

Printed in the United States of America   ISBN 0-15-372901-5

SENIOR PROGRAM ADVISERS

John F. Barbini, Ed.D.
Assistant Superintendent
School District 54
Schaumberg, Illinois

Sister Marijon Binder
Global Concerns Center
Chicago, Illinois

Paul S. Hanson
Social Studies Supervisor
Dade County Public Schools
Miami, Florida

Cheryl Biles Moore
Director, Staff Development,
  Research and Evaluation
Orange County Department of Education
Costa Mesa, California

William D. Travis, Ed.D.
Curriculum Director
Pittsfield Public Schools
Pittsfield, Massachusetts

Donald P. Vetter
Supervisor of Social Studies
Carroll County Public Schools
Westminster, Maryland

Thomas Gregory Ward
Social Studies Specialist
Fairfax County Schools, Area II
Fairfax, Virginia

Alice Wells
Curriculum Consultant
Cartwright School District No. 83
Phoenix, Arizona

SENIOR CONTENT SPECIALISTS

Biliana Cicin-Sain, Ph.D.
Associate Professor of Political Science
University of California
Santa Barbara, California

Irving Cutler, Ph.D.
Chairman Emeritus, Geography Department
Chicago State University
Chicago, Illinois

Donald O. Schneider, Ph.D.
Professor and Head of
  Social Science Education
University of Georgia
Athens, Georgia

Wm. Doyle Smith, Ph.D.
Professor of Economics
University of Texas at El Paso
El Paso, Texas

Peter J. Stein, Ph.D.
Professor of Sociology
William Paterson College
Wayne, New Jersey

SKILLS DEVELOPMENT

H. Michael Hartoonian, Ph.D.
Supervisor of Social Studies Education
Wisconsin Department of Public Instruction
Madison, Wisconsin

CLASSROOM CONSULTANTS

Judith Schrage Berg
Bamber Valley Elementary School
Rochester, Minnesota

Karen Brasch
Ellsworth Elementary School
Vancouver, Washington

Mary Brigman
Manning Primary School
Manning, South Carolina

Sally Brown
Central School
Glen Rock, New Jersey

Delores H. Casey
#2 Benjamin Harrison School
Indianapolis, Indiana

Mrs. Valerie Chevalier
Beekman Elementary School
Poughquag, New York

Jo Ann Church
College Park School
Wilmington, North Carolina

Jennifer Jenkins Cooley
Taylorsville Elementary
Taylorsville, Mississippi

Thresea A. Courtney
Austin Independent School District
Austin, Texas

Anna M. Flores
Lamar Elementary School
Corpus Christi, Texas

Helen Howland
Irving School
Duncan, Oklahoma

Junko Kako
John Swett Elementary School
Oakland, California

Peggy Lawson
Pine Tree Primary School
Longview, Texas

Sandra Levenson
Stephen Foster Elementary School
Fort Lauderdale, Florida

Diane Loughlin
Antioch C.C. School District 34
Antioch, Illinois

Emilie Paille
Douglas County Schools
Douglasville, Georgia

Karen Ann Ricketts
Central Elementary School
Flushing, Michigan

Kathy G. Walker
Highland Springs Elementary School
Highland Springs, Virginia

Susan Watkins
Cypress Fairbanks
Independent School District
Houston, Texas

Peggy Wegner
Erie School
Elyria, Ohio

Beverly Westbrook
Shenandoah Elementary School
San Antonio, Texas

Contents

List of Maps and Globes

Unit One

About You

1 Getting to Know You

3

4

2 All Around You

3 Growing and Learning

How much have you grown?

Once you were a baby.

You had to **learn** many things.

You learned to talk.

You learned to walk.

Now you can do many things.
Who helped you learn?

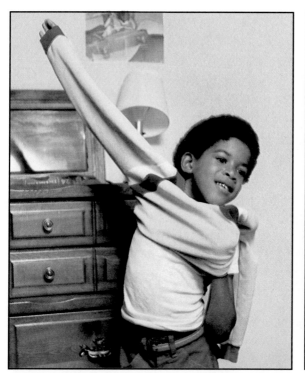

What things have you learned?

4 Living with Other People

You learned to **share.**

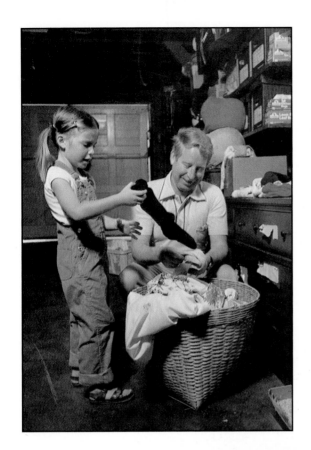

You learned to help people.

You learned to care for people.

5 Starting School

One day you started **school.**
Some children start school in August.
Some children start school in September.

You and your friends go to school together.
Sometimes you work together.

Sometimes you play together.
There are many things to do at school.

6 Learning New Things

You are learning to do many things.
You are learning to **count.**

You are learning to write.

You are learning to read.
What other new things are you learning?

7 Helpers and Leaders

There are many people at school who help you.

They help you get to school.

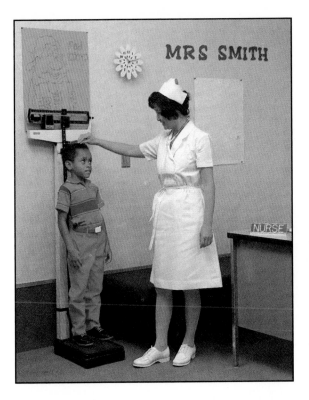

They help you in school.

The **principal** also helps you.
The principal is the **leader** of the
whole school.

Your teacher leads your class.
If you need help, you can ask your
teacher.

Alike and Different

These boxes are **alike.**

One box is **different.**
Which box is different?
How is it different?

How are these boxes different?

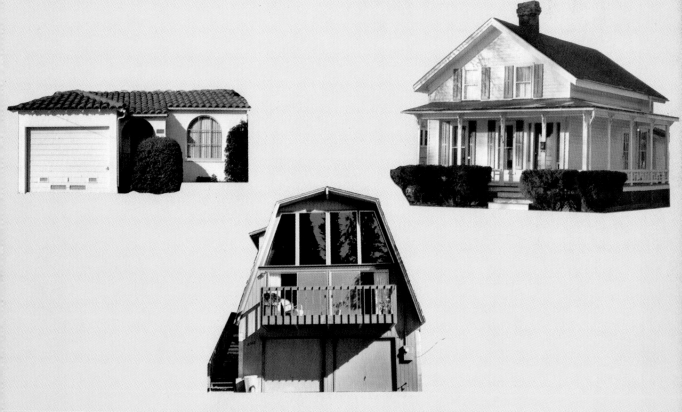

How are these houses alike?

How are they different?

What Is It Used For?

Look at these five things.
They are different in some ways.
How are they different?

These things are also alike in some ways.
They are used in games.
They are used for fun.
How else are they alike?

Here are four things that look different.

They are alike in some ways.

They are used in some of the same ways.

How are they used?

Now look at these three things.

How are they different?

How are they alike?

How do we use them?

What do we call them?

SKILLS PRACTICE

Where Is It?

Look at the picture. Then answer the questions.

1. The bookcase is to the right of the desk. What is to the left of the flag?

2. The wastebasket is in front of the desk. Who is behind the desk?

3. The bookcase is below the chalkboard. What is above the chalkboard?

4. Books are on the top shelf of the bookcase. What is on the bottom shelf?

5. The desk is between the teacher and the wastebasket. Is the door between the bookcase and the teacher?

CLOSE-UP

WHO AM I?

My friends and I go to school.

We are alike.

We are different.

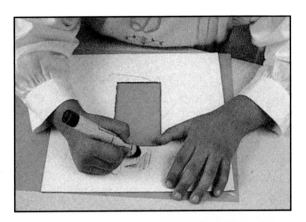

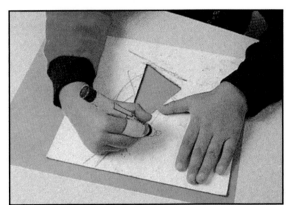

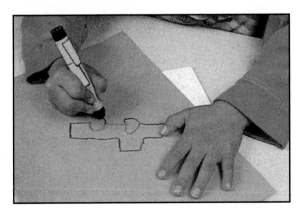

We make things with our hands.

How are our hands alike?

How are they different?

33

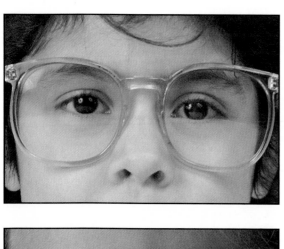
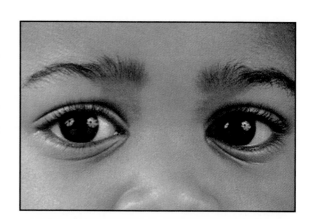

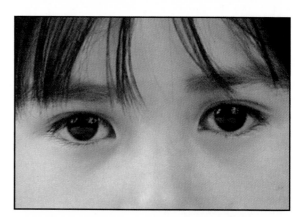

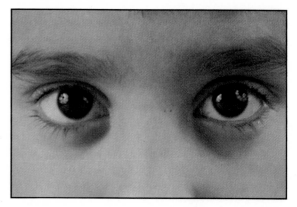

We read with our eyes.

How are our eyes alike?

How are they different?

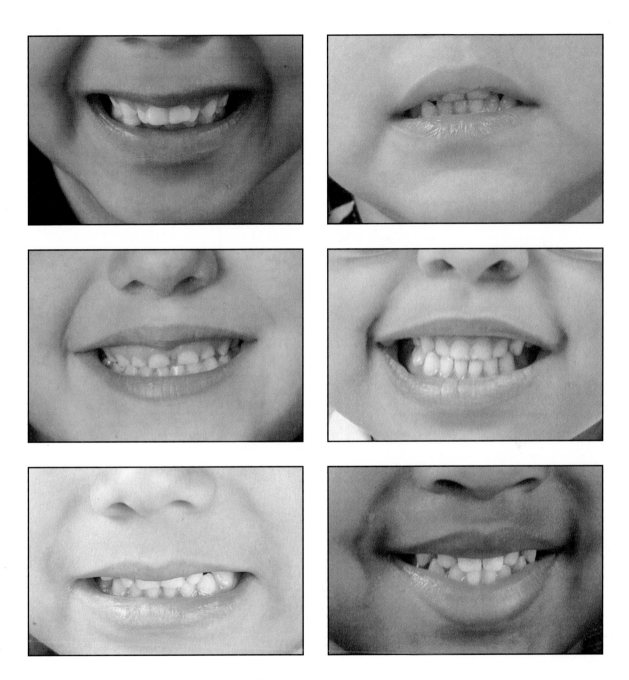

We smile with our mouths.
Are our mouths alike?
Which mouth is like yours?

35

Words

Match the words and the pictures.

1. grow
2. share
3. care
4. count
5. write
6. read

a.

b.

c.

d.

e.

f.

Thoughts

1. What do you learn at home?

2. What do you learn at school?

3. Who helps you?

4. How are you special? 🦉

Skills

1. Which things are alike? Which are different?

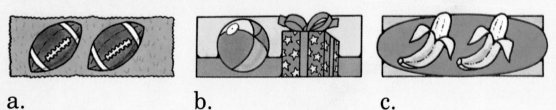

a.   b.   c.

2. Which things are used in the same way?

a.   b.   c.

3. Look at the picture. Then answer the questions.

     a. Is the car to the left of the house?

     b. Is the house behind the girl?

     c. Is the girl in front of the house?

     d. Is the kite below the boy?

     e. Is the dog between the boy and the girl?

Unit Two

About Families

1 Every Family Is Different

Some **families** are large.

Some families are smaller.

How many people are in these families?

2 Our Families Give Us Homes

We all need a place to live.

Families live in many different kinds of homes.

3 Our Families Give Us Other Things We Need

Our families give us food.

Where do our families get food?

Our families give us the clothes we need.
We need many different kinds of clothes.
Where do we get our clothes?

Our families give us love, too.
How do families show love?

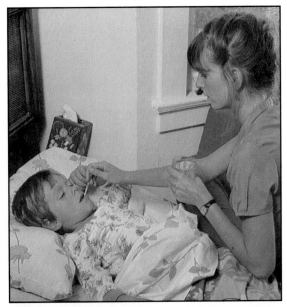

4 Families Work and Play Together

We share **work** with our families.

We help each other.

We learn from each other.
We learn new things together.

Families have fun together.

5 Families Have Rules

Rules tell us what we should do.
Rules also tell us what we should not do.
Every family has rules.
Different families have different rules.

Some rules teach us good table manners.

Some rules tell us when
we can watch TV.

Some rules are about
bedtime.

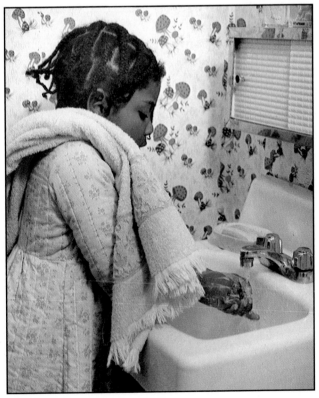

Families have rules about other people's things.

Families have rules about **safety.**

Families have rules about pets, too.

6 Schools Have Rules

Rules at school help you learn.
Rules also keep you safe.

Rules keep
things **fair.**

Following rules
shows you care
about other people.

Comparing Views

This is a picture of David's street.

David is going into his house.

What else do you see in the picture?

This is also a picture of David's street.
It shows how things look from above.
Find David and his house.
What else can you find?

SKILLS PRACTICE

Understanding Maps and Symbols

This is a **map** of David's street.

A map is a picture of a place.

How is the map like the picture on page 59?

How is it different?

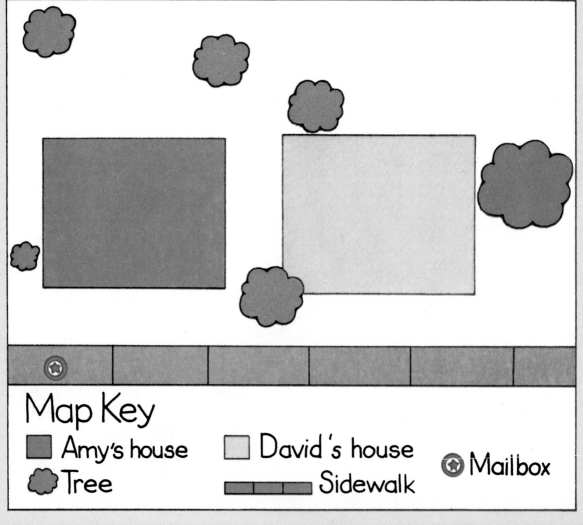

Map Key

■ Amy's house □ David's house ⊛ Mailbox

❀ Tree ▬▬▬ Sidewalk

Maps use **symbols.**

Symbols are small drawings of real things.

Symbols can be any shape or color.

Do these symbols look the same as the pictures?

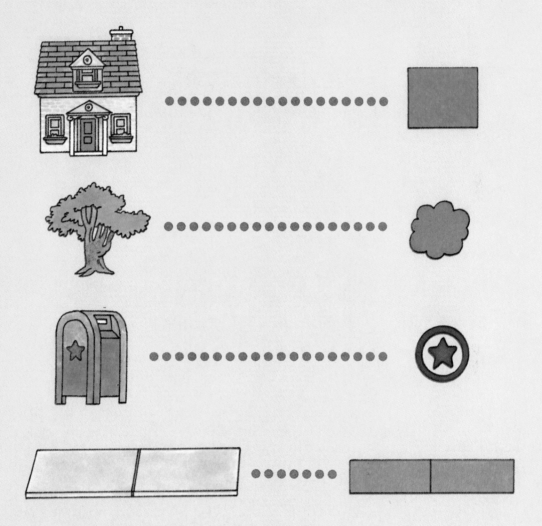

A **map key** tells what each symbol stands for.

Find the map key on the map.

On the map key, find the symbol for a tree.

How many trees are there on the map?

Now find the other symbols on the map.

Map Key

Store | Tree | Park

School | House | Road

Here is another map.

Look at the map and the map key.
Then answer the questions.

1. What is in the middle of the map?

2. How many houses are there?

3. How many stores are there?

4. What is between the school and the houses?

5. What is behind the school?

6. Which road is in front of the school?

Using a Classroom Map

This is a map of a classroom.

Look at the map and the map key.

How many pupils are in this classroom?

What is between the pupils' desks and the chalkboard?

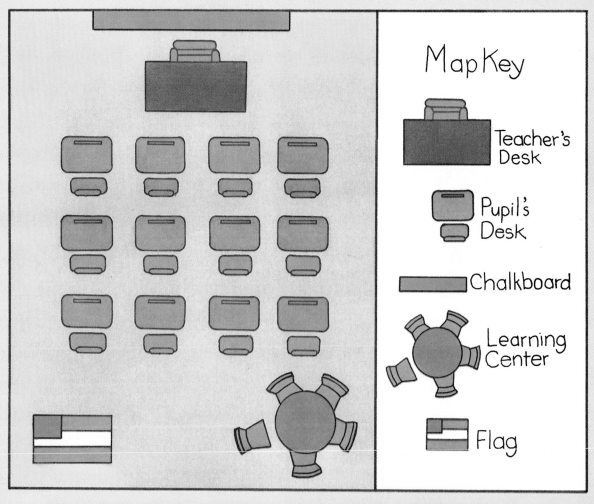

Map Key

Teacher's Desk

Pupil's Desk

Chalkboard

Learning Center

Flag

SKILLS PRACTICE

Finding Your Way at School

This is a map of a school.

Look at the map and the map key.

What can you find on this map?

How is this map like the map on page 64?

How is it different?

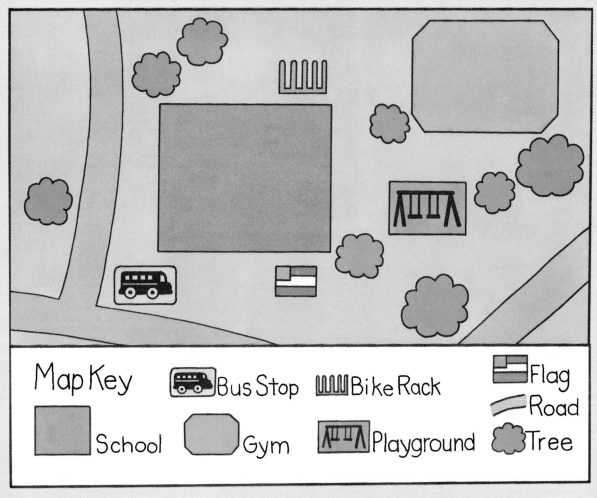

Map Key

Bus Stop

Bike Rack

Flag

School

Gym

Playground

Road

Tree

CLOSE-UP

WHERE DO YOU LIVE?

Freddy lives on top of a store.
His father owns the store.

Tanya's home is tall.
It was a lighthouse.

Nora lives on a boat.
Her yard is a lake.

67

Vincent lives in a log cabin.
It is far from the city.

Victoria's home is in a hill.
It is warm in winter.
It is cool in summer.

68

Sam's home is round.

It is a hogan.

Paula's home is also round.

It is a dome.

Which home is like your home?

69

Words

Match the words and the pictures.

1. family
2. rule
3. map
4. symbol
5. map key

a.

b.

c.

d.

e.

Thoughts

1. How are families different?

2. What are four things our families give us?

3. What are three things families do together?

4. Why do you follow rules?

Skills

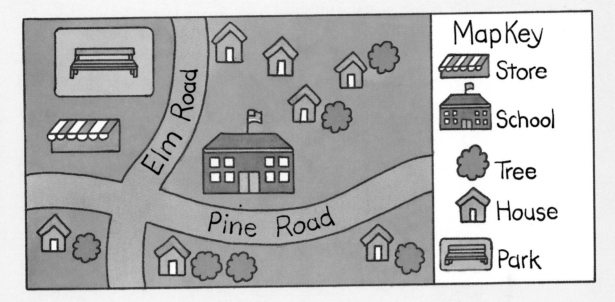

Look at the map and the map key.
Then answer the questions.

1. What is in the middle of the map?

2. How many stores are there?

3. What is between the park and the school?

4. What is behind the store?

Activities

Draw a map of your classroom or your bedroom.
Draw a map key to go with it.

Needs and Wants

1 People Have Needs

Needs are things people must have.
Our families need a place to live.
We need food to eat and water to drink.

74

We need clothes to keep
us warm and dry.

Some clothes help keep
us cool when it is hot.

What other needs do
people have?

2 People Have Wants

Wants are things that people would like to have.

Families cannot always have everything
they want.
They must choose what they want most.

3 What Do People Buy?

People buy things they need and want.
They use **money** to pay for things.

Look at what this family is buying.
Which are needs?
Which are wants?

People spend money in different ways.

They buy things that will last a long time.

They buy things they really need.

4 Working for What We Need and Want

People must work to earn money.
People use money to buy things.
People work in many different places.
They work inside and outside.

Some people work alone.

Many people work with other people.

People have many different kinds of jobs.
Sometimes their jobs help other people.
Jobs that help others are called **services.**
How are these people helping?

Some people make things.

Things people make are called **goods.**

What goods are these people making?

5 Children Work, Too

Sometimes children have jobs.
They work to buy the things they want.

What jobs do these young people have?

SKILLS PRACTICE

Making Lists

Why do we make **lists?**

Sometimes we make lists for fun.

We make lists of things we like.

Sometimes we need to remember things.

Lists help us remember.

Which things do not belong on these lists?

Things to buy at the grocery store	Things I like to do
1. bread	1. sing
2. a haircut	2. swim
3. oranges	3. play ball
4. milk	4. pencils

SKILLS PRACTICE

Which Are Needs and Which Are Wants?

Needs are things that are important.
Needs are important for life and health.

Wants are things that are nice to have.
Wants are things we can live without.

Look at these two lists.

1. Which list shows needs?

2. Which list shows wants?

3. How would you finish these lists?

1. place to live	1. puzzle
2. food	2. roller skates
3. love	3. pony ride
4. ?	4. ?

SKILLS PRACTICE

People at Work

Who are these workers? What are they doing?

1.

2.

3.

4.

5.

6.

What do the workers need to do their jobs?

Match the workers with the things they use
  at work.

a.

b.

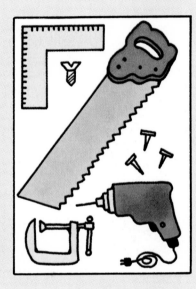

c.

d.

e.

f.

Maps show where things are.
This is a map of a shopping center.
People buy things at shopping centers.

Look at the map. Then answer the questions.

1. Is the bookstore next to the parking lot?

2. Is the pet store next to the bookstore?

3. Which store is next to the toy store?

4. Which store is between the parking lot and the bookstore?

5. Which store is between the toy store and the grocery store?

CLOSE-UP

CHILDREN'S JOBS

Alicia's family grows fruit.
Alicia helps pick the fruit.
She also helps sell it.

Bobby's mother rents rooms.

Bobby helps her clean the rooms.

Lee's father takes care of plants.

Lee helps him water the plants.

93

Cara's family has a fish farm.
She helps feed the fish.
Stores buy the fish.

Jane's mother makes dolls.
Jane puts clothes on the dolls.
They sell the dolls at craft fairs.

Keith's family sells goods.

They sell at a flea market.

Keith helps keep the goods neat.

Words

Use these words to finish the sentences.

money	wants	goods	needs	buy

1. _____ are things we cannot live without.

2. _____ are things we would like to have.

3. _____ are things people make.

4. People _____ things they need and want.

5. People use _____ to pay for things.

Thoughts

1. What are three needs that all people have?

2. Name two services. What workers do these jobs?

3. Name two goods. What workers make these goods?

4. Name two jobs that you could do.

Skills

Look at the pictures.

1. Make a list of the things that are needs.

2. Make a list of the things that are wants.

house   skates   milk   shoes

glove   flowers   paints   fruit

Look at the map. Then answer the questions.

1. Is the shoe store next to the bookstore?

2. Which store is next to the toy store?

3. Which store is between the toy store and the grocery store?

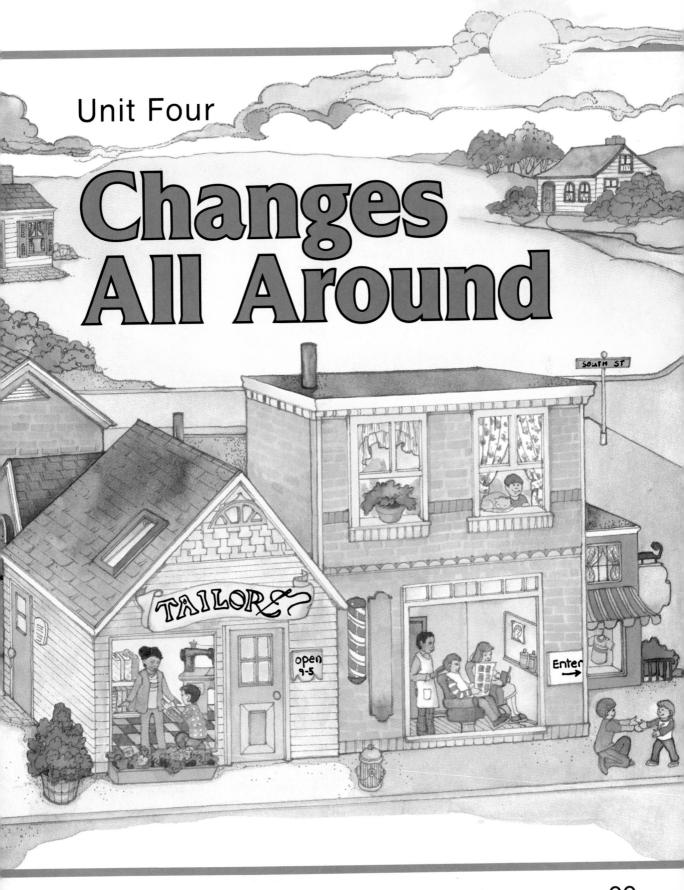

Unit Four

Changes All Around

1 Families Make Changes

Families **change.**

How are these families changing?

2 Seasons Bring Changes

Places change during the year.
Every **season** is different.
How is this farm changing?

Spring

Summer

Fall

Winter

How do the seasons change where you live?

3 Our Neighborhoods Change

Some **neighborhoods** do not stay the same.

People take down old buildings.

People build new buildings.

Sometimes old buildings are used in new ways.

4 Towns Change, Too

Towns do not always stay the same.
This is Rivertown long ago.

Rivertown changed into a **city.**

What changes do you see?

SKILLS PRACTICE

Day and Night

Look at the pictures. Then answer the questions.

1. Which things are happening in the morning?

2. Which things are happening in the afternoon?

3. Which things are happening at night?

a.

b.

c.

d.

e.

f.

SKILLS PRACTICE

What Time Is It?

Choose the right time.

1. When does this boy get up?

a.   b.

2. When do these children eat lunch?

a.   b.

3. When do these children go home from school?

a. 9 30   b. 2 30

4. When does this family eat dinner?

a.   b. 6 00

Which clocks show the same time?

1. 9 30   2. 3 00

3.

4.

The Days of the Week

There are seven days in a week.
Sunday is the first day.

Sunday	Monday	Tuesday	Wednesday	Thursday	Friday	Saturday
1	2	3	4	5	6	7
		I rode my bike.	Today I am playing baseball.	I will play soccer.		

Look at the pictures. Then answer the questions.

1. What is the last day of the week?

2. What day comes after Tuesday?

3. What day comes after Thursday?

4. What did Daniel do on Tuesday?

5. What will Daniel do on Thursday?

110

Past, Present, and Future

Things happening now are in the present.
Things that have already happened are
  in the past.
Things that are going to happen are in
  the future.

This is Anna in
  the present.

Which pictures show Anna in the past?
Which pictures show Anna in the future?

1.   2.   3.   4.

Maps Can Show Changes

Maps can show how neighborhoods change.
This map shows Lisa's neighborhood
    long ago.

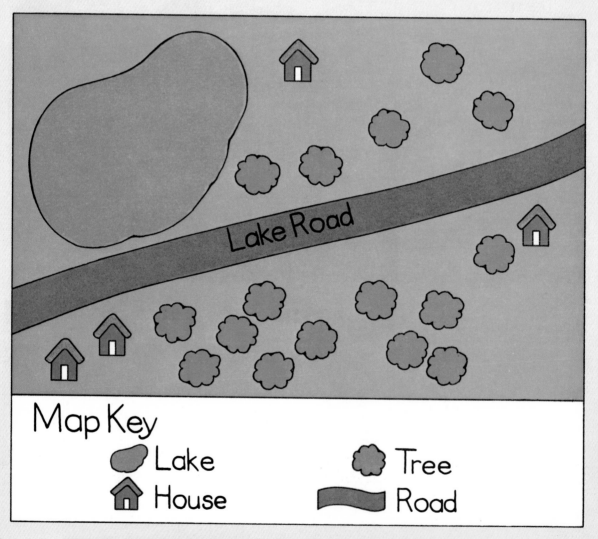

Map Key

Lake

House

Tree

Road

This map shows Lisa's neighborhood today.
How has Lisa's neighborhood changed?
How has it stayed the same?

Lake Road

Map Key
Lake
Tree
House
Store
School
Road

CLOSE-UP

HOW COWBOYS HAVE CHANGED

These are pictures of early Texas cowboys.

114

The first Texas cowboys were
Mexican.
They helped teach other cowboys to
take care of cows.
All cowboys rode horses.

Cowboys put a brand on each cow.
Each ranch has a brand.
It tells who owns the cow.
Cowboys still brand cows today.

115

Cowboys took cows from Texas to
 towns with a train stop.
This trip was called a trail drive.
Cows from many ranches went on the
 trail drive.

The cows went by train to other states.
They were sold for food.

116

Today cows are sent from Texas to
other states in trucks.

Cowboys still ride horses.
They also ride in other things.

117

Words

Match the words and the pictures.

1. change
2. seasons
3. neighborhood
4. city
5. week

a.

b.

c.

d.

e.

Thoughts

1. How do families change? Name two ways.

2. What are the four seasons?

3. How are the seasons different where you live?

4. How do neighborhoods change? Name two ways.

5. How has your town changed? 🦉

Skills

What time is it? How can you tell?

1.   2.   3.

What day comes next?

1. Monday   2. Wednesday   3. Friday
   Tuesday   Thursday   Saturday
   [?]   [?]   [?]

Activities

1. Draw a picture. Show two things you
   do during the day. Write the times on
   your picture.

2. What do you want to do in the future?
   Tell about something you want to learn.

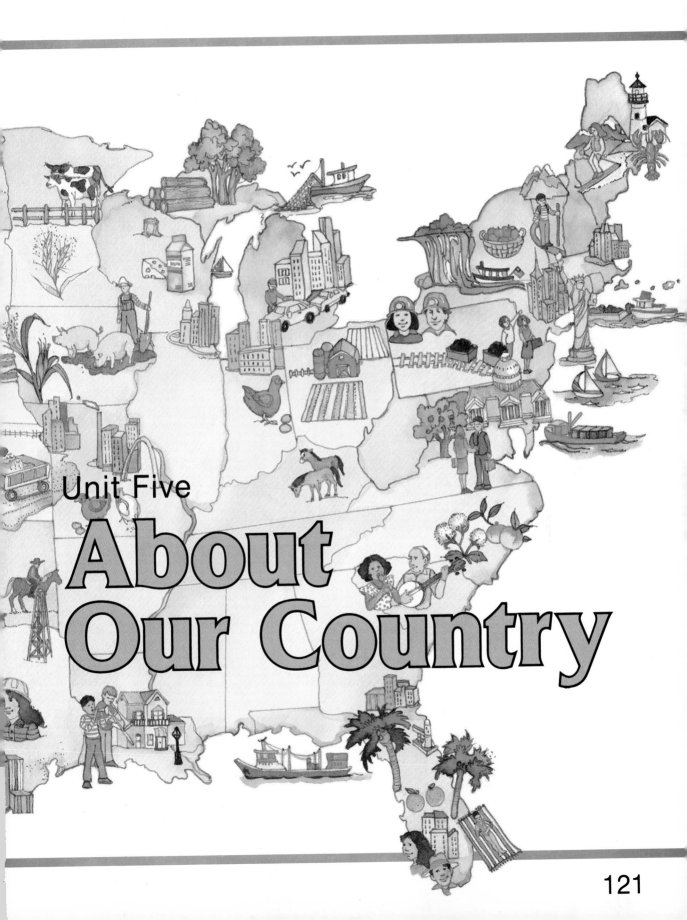

Unit Five

About Our Country

1 The American People

We are all **Americans.**

We live in the **United States of America.**

Americans are different in many ways.
Americans are alike in many ways, too.

2 The United States

The United States is a big country.

Our country has many beautiful places.
We work to keep these places clean.
We try to keep them beautiful.

The United States has many big cities.
Many Americans live in these cities.

Other Americans live in small towns.

Other Americans live on **farms.**
They grow the food that we all need.

3 Our Country's Resources

Our country has many **resources.**

Resources are things that people use.

Trees and water are resources.

Oil and land are resources, too.

Resources are used to
make things we need.

We must use our resources
carefully.
We want them to last a
long time.

4 Our Country's Past

Indians were the first Americans.
They lived in all parts of the United States.
They lived in many kinds of homes.

In 1492 Christopher Columbus came to America.
He told people about the land he had found.
Then other people came to America.

This picture shows the Pilgrims.

They came to America long ago.

Their first year was hard.

The Indians helped them.

The Indians and the Pilgrims
shared a big dinner.

It was the first Thanksgiving.

Other people came to America.

They came from many different countries.

They sailed across the ocean in small ships.

They built houses.

They planted **crops.**

They worked hard in their new country.

5 Remembering Our Country's Past

The United States once belonged to a
country called England.
Americans wanted to be free.
They fought to have their own country.
We **celebrate** this on Independence Day.
It is our country's birthday.

On Independence Day we honor our **flag.**

It stands for the United States.

We honor our flag on many other days, too.

Remembering Our Country's Leaders

Many people have helped our country. We remember these people on their birthdays.

George Washington was our first **President.** He fought for our country's freedom. His birthday is on February 22.

Abraham Lincoln was a President, too. He kept our country together. He helped all Americans become free. His birthday is on February 12.

Long ago, women could not vote.
Susan B. Anthony helped change
    that.
Today, American women can vote.
February 15 is Susan B. Anthony
    Day.

This is a picture of Martin
    Luther King, Jr.
He helped change our country.
He helped make it more fair.
We honor Martin Luther King
    on January 15.

Living and Working Together

People belong to many **groups.**

These people are in the same family.

These children go to the same school.

These children live in the same neighborhood.

We all live in the same country.

How can we be good group members?

We follow rules.

We share.

We help each other.

We listen.

We are polite.

We work together.

Look at these people.
How are they being good family members?

Our School

How can we be good members of our school?

We follow the rules.

How are these children being good school members?

Our Neighborhoods

We must all be good neighbors.

How are these people being good neighbors?

Our Country

How can we be good Americans?

We keep our country clean.

We learn about our country.   We obey its rules.

How else can we be good Americans?

SKILLS PRACTICE

A Map of the United States

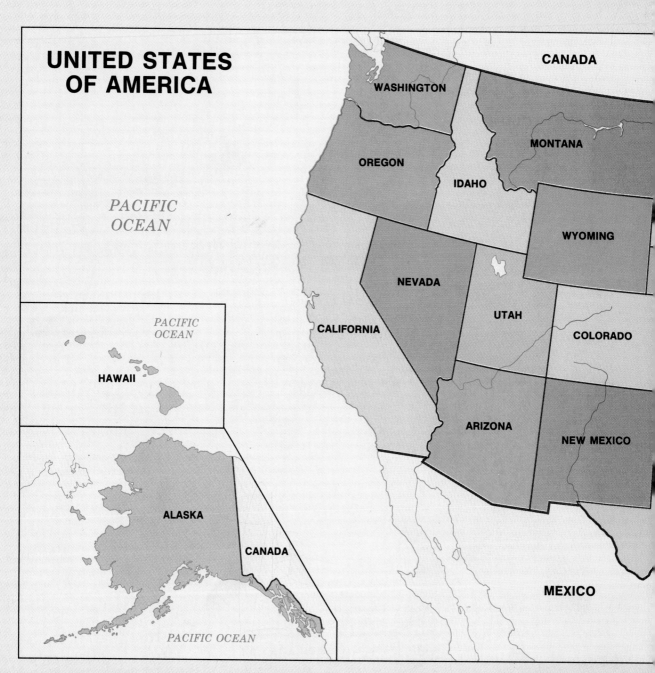

UNITED STATES OF AMERICA

CANADA

WASHINGTON

MONTANA

PACIFIC OCEAN

OREGON

IDAHO

WYOMING

NEVADA

UTAH

COLORADO

CALIFORNIA

PACIFIC OCEAN

HAWAII

ARIZONA

NEW MEXICO

ALASKA

CANADA

MEXICO

PACIFIC OCEAN

144

Maps can show very big places.
This is a map of the United States.
It shows the 50 parts of our country.
Each part is called a **state.**
Can you find your state on the map?

CLOSE-UP

HOW OUR FLAG IS MADE

Many families fly the American flag.
Some fly it on holidays.
Some fly it every day.
They fly it in front of their homes.

146

American flags are made in a factory.
Other flags are made here also.

A worker sews stars on blue cloth.

147

Another worker sews the red and white stripes together.

Then a worker sews the stars and stripes together. Sometimes our flag is called the Stars and Stripes.

148

Do you have a flag?

Fly it outdoors in good weather.

Take it off the flag pole at night.

Fold the flag carefully.

Do not let it touch the ground.

You honor the flag when you follow these rules.

149

UNIT 5 REVIEW

Words

Use these words to finish the sentences.

crops	Independence Day	groups
resource	Thanksgiving	

1. Trees are a _____.

2. The Pilgrims and Indians had the first _____.

3. Farmers plant _____.

4. We celebrate our country's freedom on _____.

5. We all belong to many _____.

Thoughts

1. Who were the first Americans?

2. Who were the Pilgrims?

3. What does our flag stand for?

4. Why do we celebrate Thanksgiving?

Skills

Match the sentences and the pictures.

1. We listen and are polite.

2. We put things away.

3. We keep our country clean.

4. We take turns.

5. We help each other.

6. We learn about our country.

a.

b.

c.

d.

e.

f.

Activities

1. List three of the rules in your school.

2. Look at the map of our country on pages 144 and 145. Find your state. Name a state that is next to your state. Name a state that is far from your state.

CHINA

CANADA

USA

NIGERIA

152

A Look at the World

1 Our Country and the World

The United States is our country.

There are many countries in the **world.**

Every country is different.

No two countries look alike.

No two countries have the same past.

The people of every country are different, too.
They have their own ways of doing things.

Mexico

China

Nigeria

2 How Are People Alike?

Families all over the world have the same
  needs.
We all need homes to live in.

Nigeria

Mexico

China

Canada

China

Canada

We all need food.

We all need clothes.

We all need love from our families and friends.

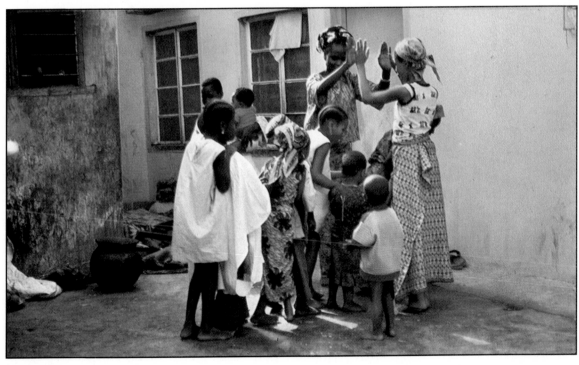

Nigeria

We must work to get the things we need.
People all over the world do many of the
same jobs.
What are these people doing?

China

Canada

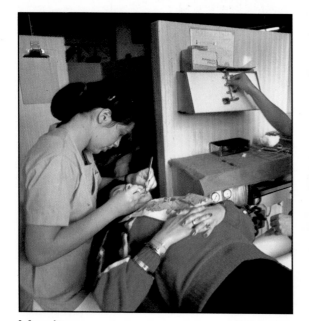

Mexico

Nigeria

3 The Changing World

The world is always changing.
People change the land.
People use resources.
Cities grow larger.

Canada

China

People learn new ways of doing things.

They share what they know.

Nigeria

China

Just like you, people everywhere grow
and change.

160

4 Holidays Around the World

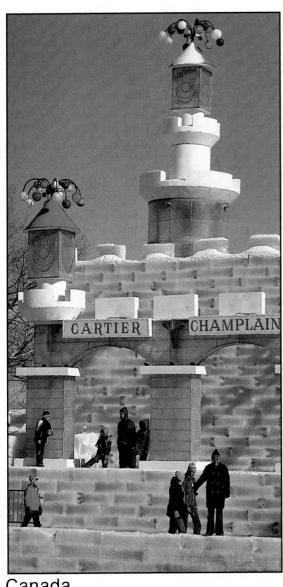
Canada

Nigeria

People all over the world have **holidays.**
Holidays are times for sharing fun.

China

In China, Spring Festival is an
  important holiday.
Spring Festival begins the new year
  in China.
People go to parades.
Everyone wishes for good luck in the new year.

Mexico once belonged to a country called Spain.

Today Mexico is a free country.

Mexicans celebrate their Independence Day
in September.

Mexico

At night they watch fireworks.

The next day they have parties and parades.

How is their Independence Day like ours?

163

What Is a Globe?

A **model** is a small copy of something.

Picture 1 shows a model of an airplane.

Picture 2 shows a real airplane.

Which other pictures show models?

1.

2.

3.

4.

5.

6.

This is a picture of the
Earth.

The girl is looking at
a **globe.**
A globe is a small model
of the Earth.
The globe is the same
shape as the Earth.
What shape is it?

SKILLS PRACTICE

What Globes Show

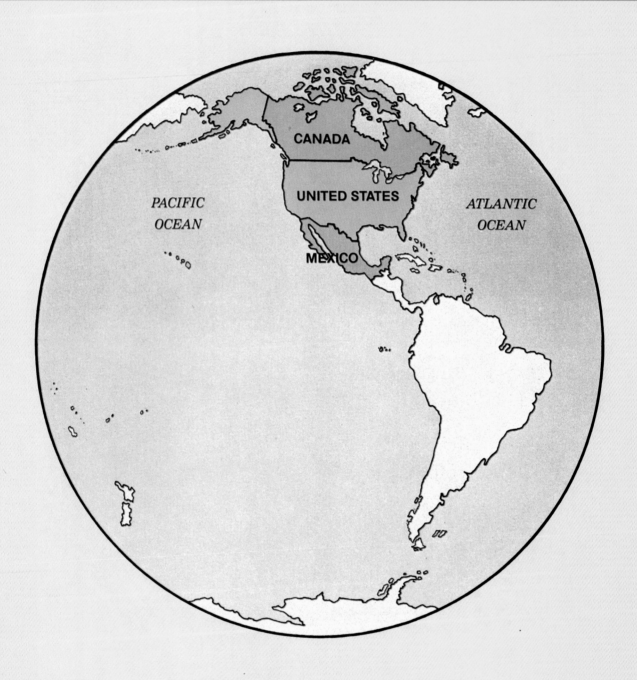

Globes show land and water.

Land is many different colors.

What color is water?

Look at the globe. Then answer the questions.

1. Find the Atlantic Ocean. What other
   ocean can you find?

2. Find the United States. What other
   countries can you find?

SKILLS PRACTICE
Learning About Directions

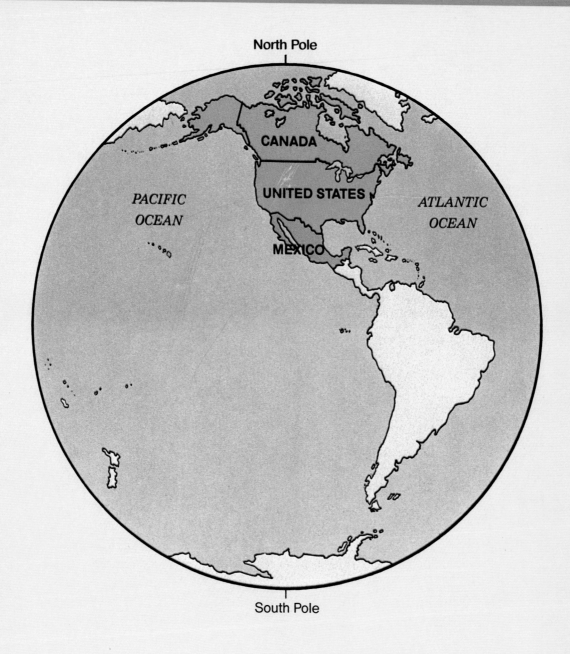

North Pole

CANADA

UNITED STATES

PACIFIC OCEAN

ATLANTIC OCEAN

MEXICO

South Pole

Globes show more than land and water.
Globes show the **North Pole** and the **South Pole.**

Find the United States on the globe.
Find the North Pole.
Put your finger on the United States.
Now move your finger toward the North Pole.
You are moving north.

Find the South Pole.
Put your finger on the United States.
Now move your finger toward the South Pole.
You are moving south.

Is Canada north or south of the United States?
Is Mexico north or south of the United States?

CLOSE-UP

HORSES AROUND THE WORLD

People all over the world
ride horses.
The first horses were too
small to ride.
They were only as tall as
this book.

170

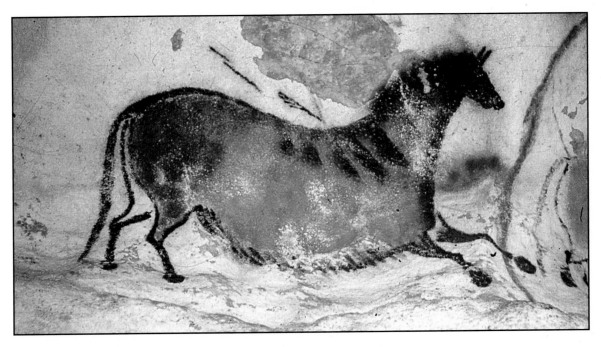

Long ago horses were wild.

Then horses were tamed.

People rode horses to hunt for food.

They rode horses to fight.

171

People rode horses to play.

They rode horses to go places.

Horses helped people work.

Many children ride horses.

Which horse can you ride?

173

Words

Match the words and the pictures.

1. world
2. holiday
3. model
4. globe
5. poles

a.

b.

c.

d.

e.

Thoughts

1. In what ways are the people of the world alike?

2. What do people do on holidays?

3. Why are holidays important?

Skills

Look at the globe. Then answer the questions.

1. What letter is on the United States?

2. What letter is on the North Pole?

3. What letter is on Mexico?

4. What letter is on the Atlantic Ocean?

Activities

Look at a globe. Name the country that is north of the United States. Name two countries that are south of Canada.

ATLAS

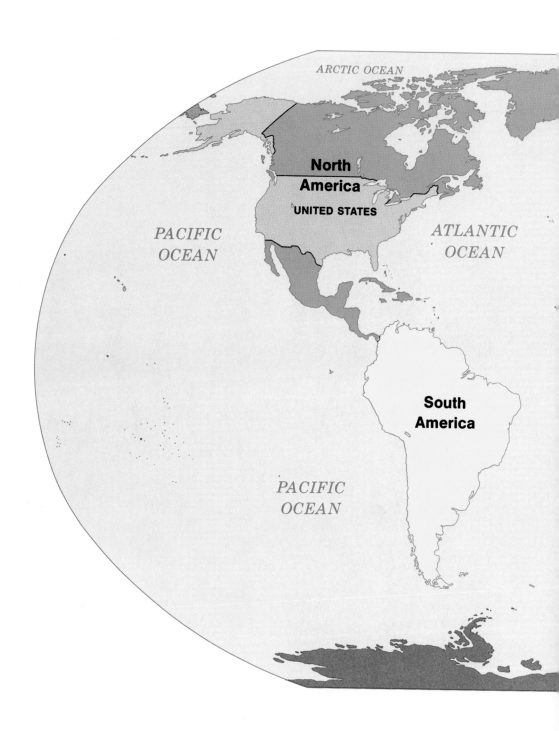

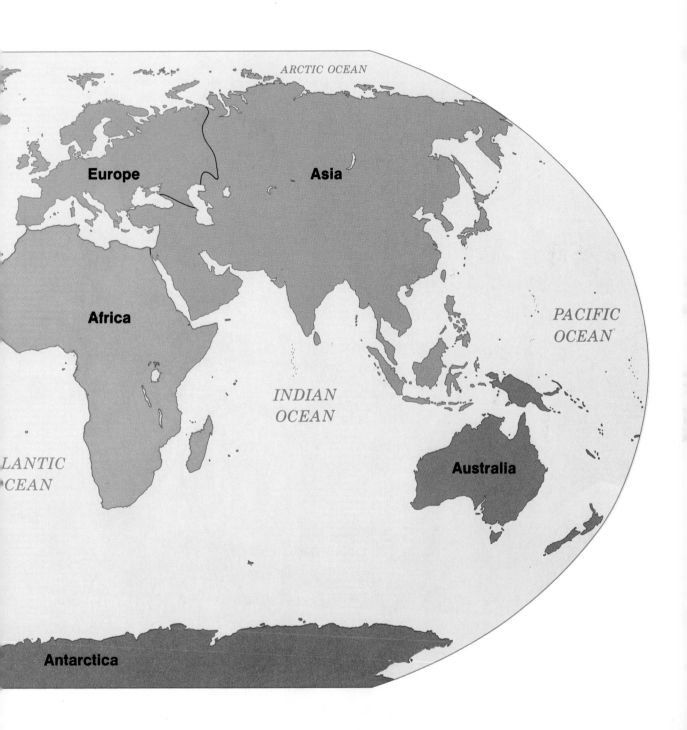

The Pledge of Allegiance

I pledge allegiance
to the flag of the United
States of America and to the
Republic for which it stands,
one Nation under God,
indivisible, with liberty
and justice for all.

PICTURE GLOSSARY

alike (p. 26)

Americans (p. 122)

celebrate (p. 134)

change (p. 100)

city (p. 107)

count (p. 19)

crops (p. 133)

different (p. 26)

Earth (p. 165)

fair (p. 57)

family (p. 40)

farm (p. 127)

flag (p. 135)

globe (p. 165)

goods (p. 83)

group (p. 138)

holiday (p. 161)

leader (p. 24)

learn (p. 11)

list (p. 86)

map (p. 60)

map key (p. 61)

House
Tree
School

model (p. 164)

money (p. 78)

needs (p. 74)

neighborhood (p. 104)

North Pole (p. 169)

President (p. 136)

principal (p. 24)

resources (p. 128)

rule (p. 52)

safety (p. 55)

school (p. 17)

seasons (p. 102)

service (p. 82)

share (p. 14)

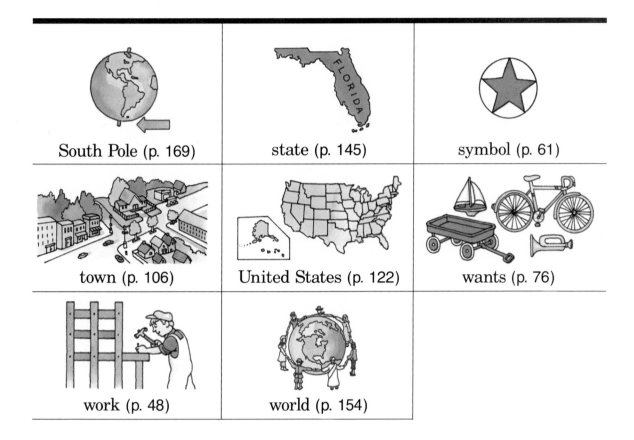

South Pole (p. 169)

state (p. 145)

symbol (p. 61)

town (p. 106)

United States (p. 122)

wants (p. 76)

work (p. 48)

world (p. 154)

Photographs

Key: T, Top; B, Bottom; L, Left; C, Center; R, Right.

Illustrations

Maps